Marketing Automation

B. Vincent

Published by RWG Publishing, 2021.

MARKETING AUTOMATION

First edition. June 16, 2021.

Written by B. Vincent.

Table of Contents

Also by B. Vincent

Marketing Automation

Hello and welcome to this course on **Marketing Automation**. In this course, we're going to cover how to increase your sales by leveraging automation workflows. This course is divided into three modules, *Module 1* is an overview of automation, concepts, and tools, *Module 2* covers common automation workflows, and campaigns and *Module 3* teaches you how to build your first workflow from scratch. By the time this course is over, you'll know how to effectively use your marketing automation for your business. So without further ado, let's dive into the first module. Okay guys, welcome to Module 1, in this module, our expert will give us an overview of automation concepts, and tools, so get ready to take some notes, and let's jump right in.

Module 1

All right, so for starters, what is marketing automation? Well, the textbook definition sounds something like this, it's a process where technology is used to automate several repetitive tasks that are undertaken on a regular basis in a marketing campaign. That's true, but today, when people refer to automation and online marketing, they're usually referring to specifically workflows that use smart logic to take action based on how prospects behave or other parameters. Basically marketing automation today means using technology to dynamically adapt the experience of your prospects, your leads or your customers after their initial reaction to your business, based on either their actions or other attributes about them. For example, once a lead opts into an email list, you can customize a subsequent marketing message sent to them based on their location. Or maybe based on answers that they filled out on a form or based on whether or not they've opened certain emails, clicked certain links, visited certain pages and so on and so forth. In fact, you could even dig down so deep that you tailor your marketing messages based on how long they watched a video before leaving the video. That's how in-depth this whole concept of marketing automation has gotten these days. Does that make sense? So we're going to go more in-depth into the types of automation workflows that you can create later on. There's a whole bunch of them, but first let's familiarize ourselves with the various tools that you can use to leverage marketing automation in your business.

The first two that we're going to look at are email specific, they mostly center around email automation, which is probably the vast majority of marketing automation that happens today. That's going to be Drip and GetResponse. Drip is a very cool, slightly newer email-marketing platform, and what we're looking at right here are basically templates for their workflows. You can get really into the weeds and take all sorts of specific actions based on how they're behaving and how they're responding to your marketing campaigns. And the marketing automation is probably one of the more powerful features of Drip, it's one of the things that they focused on when they first came into existence not too long ago. As you can see right here, there's a little diagram of the marketing automation and workflows that you can create. The one thing that all of these tools have in common is that they're all drag and drop these days. There's no programming involved or anything like that, it's all drag and drop, the creation of automation workflows very easily. Anybody can do it, even if you have very low-tech skills.

The next one is going to be GetResponse, and this has been around a whole lot longer. When it was first created, it was basically meant to be an automation and a newsletter broadcasting platform for email, but they also added marketing automation as a newer feature not too long ago, and it's very similar to Drip. Slightly less functionality, it's almost completely 100% email-based, whereas Drip does overlap into other things like adding people to custom Facebook audiences and integration with other applications as well. Whereas

GetResponse is almost entirely focused just on the actual emails, the meat and potatoes of email marketing and almost nothing else. Still a very good platform though, for automating your email marketing. One of the common themes that you're going to see here as you go through GetResponse is the question of tagging and scoring. As people act a certain way, as they behave a certain way in response to your emails, you're basically going to track that or the software is going to track that and it's going to assign scores. So a certain amount of points are going to be earned every time somebody opens an email, every time somebody clicks on a link and so on and so forth. And so your contacts are gradually going to actually develop, no kidding, real scores, and those scores can be used to trigger other actions down the road. For example, somebody doesn't open an email after like 20 days, there's still no email opens happening, and so their score drops to a level, where suddenly a trigger comes into play and they're sent into what's called a win-back sequence. Where you start sending specific subject lines that are designed to acknowledge that they're not opening their emails and trying to get them to open those emails and engage with you in some way, shape or form before eventually, if the score gets low enough, booting them from your list for the sake of list hygiene. That's just an example of what you can do with scoring, you get the idea though, it's very in-depth, and there's a whole lot of things that you can do.

Now, Drip and GetResponse were just two of many email marketing automation platforms that there are. Let's have a look at one of the all-in-one platforms out there. This is getting to be a more common theme these days, the all-in-one concept, instead of the best-in-class concept. It's a different philosophy and there's no right or wrong about it. Kartra is one of the more high visibility all-in-one platforms, and basically what that means is it's not just automating your marketing messages, it's also including all of your other stuff as well. So the landing pages, the opt-in pages, the sales pages, the checkout carts, the payment processing, the building of sales funnels, all that good stuff, plus all of the stuff that we just talked about on the email side of things as well. Even memberships, so product delivery, all of that sort of contained in one thing, and as you can see, it's designed to work together quite well within the platform. So lead capture page, somebody opts in here, a lead is created, they have a tag added to that lead, which is just prospect, and then they're subscribed to a campaign. Then they're sent to a sales page and after they check out, then they are untagged as prospects, and then they're tagged as a customer because now they've purchased something and you can send emails based on that behavior. And then later on, if they purchase an upsell, then they are tagged as a repeat customer, and then they're sent to the product delivery, the membership, you get the idea just on and on it goes. So many things that you can do with tagging, scoring as was the case with GetResponse, and basically just adapting the entire experience from their perspective based on their behavior and the action that they take.

Now Kartra, we called all-in-one because it includes both the front-end customer facing lead capture and sales pages and funnel aspect of things, plus the email automation side of things. And the Drip and GetResponse platforms were mostly email-related with maybe a couple of other things woven in there, but the true all-encompassing marketing automation platform is going to be Autopilot. Autopilot has got its hands in so many different bowls. It is not a funnel builder, it does not attempt to be like Kartra or like click funnels. It doesn't handle the customer facing front-end pages, but it does so much more than just email marketing. The email marketing and the marketing automation software in Autopilot reaches into Facebook ad pixels, they reaches into using Twilio for SMS messaging. It reaches into all sorts of other tools like Trello and Slack and so on and so forth. There's no end to the things that you can do inside of Autopilot. It connects with Pipedrive, is one example here, it connects with all sorts of other things. You've got your Facebook here, you've got Typeform there, there are so many different things it connects with. And because of that, you can do multifaceted automation, workflows that reach in all sorts of different directions and through all sorts of different channels. One example would be the sending of actual physical postcards, that's another thing that you can automate via Autopilot. Not many platforms can say that, and so for that reason, Autopilot is what we're going to be using as we go through the next couple of modules. We look at the types of marketing automation, workflows, and campaigns that you can create, different templates, different styles as well as finally creating our own campaign from scratch. We're going to be doing all that inside of Autopilot. Whichever platform you end up using, most of the functionality that you're trying to achieve, especially on the email automation side is going to be mostly the same. It's all click, drag and drop, some of the terminologies will be a little bit different, but it will be most of the same, so don't feel pressured to only use Autopilot. That's what we're going to be using though, because of how expansive it is.

Module 2

Hey folks, welcome to Module 2. In this module, our expert will cover common automation workflows, and campaigns, so get ready to take some notes and let's jump right in.

All right, so we're going to be starting out with the most basic of workflow automations, and that is basic lead nurturing. And again, we're using Autopilot here, we're going to be using that for all of the different types of workflows that we're going to be looking at in this module. You can do basically the same thing in any platform that you're going to be using, but Autopilot is nice for our purposes here because it includes a whole bunch of preloaded and fleshed out types of campaigns. Starting from the very basic nurturing a new lead, all the way to the more advanced stuff having to do with webinars, text messages, cart, abandonment, and that sort of thing. So let's jump straight into this one, nurturing a lead, this is very basic, very bare bones. Someone joins a certain list, when they join that list, then they're sent an email, once that email is sent, there's a delay of, in this case, 10 days, and then another email is sent. Another delay, another email sent, another delay, another email, and then once you're done sending them the content that you use for nurturing them, you would add them to a new list. In this case, the list is called <u>nurture done</u>, which could potentially start them on a whole another new automation campaign designed to fulfill another purpose. But the important thing here to know is that while all of these things are happening, it's not linear, other things are happening as well.

So this email was sent, and then there's a condition line here saying 'on click'. So if that email is clicked, they get sent into a one day delay and then they're sent another email follow-up, same thing here. So if any of the emails throughout this entire period of what looks like probably about 30 days, so nurturing a lead over the course of 30 days, if any of them are not only open, but a link inside is clicked, well that's an indicator to you that they are interested in what you're offering. And one day after clicking, any of those emails, they're sent into this whole workflow process here, which includes a sales follow-up, and here's an example of a sales follow-up. *Hi, Lisa, we noticed you're interested in learning more about trial journeys, et cetera, et cetera. Would you like to book an interactive demo?* So that's just an example of what they do over at Autopilot, that's what would be in this email. How do you know that they're interested, because they clicked. And you used your drag and drop interface to say if anybody clicks on a link inside of one of these emails, start a one day timer and then send them these follow-up sales emails. After that happens, they're added to nurture engaged, which is a new list, which again could start them on a whole other campaign, and they are ejected from this journey. Because they're already working directly with a sales representative, they're getting demos and stuff, they don't need to continue getting all of these emails. And so one of the actions that are taken based on their behavior is they're ejected after they've been added to this list. That's a very basic 101 level new lead nurturing workflow right there.

Another one we can look at though is a 30-day trial nurturing campaign. So let's say you have a software and you're letting people demo it or trial it free for 30 days, this is what you could do. First off, you'll notice as soon as someone submits a form signing up for the free trial, there are two different courses of action that begin simultaneously. First, an email is sent and we'll go down this track in a moment, but then also they're sent a message, a heads-up message, and they're added to a Facebook custom audience, which is also very handy for remarketing. Now, following up on that email, the free trial email is sent and there's a one day delay, and after that delay, another email is sent here and there are some notes to explain what's going on here. Basically the first three days of a trial is when people are most likely to open and respond to emails, so this template puts a lot of emphasis on day one, two and three, and that's why there's a short duration. There are only 24 hours of gaps in between the first several emails. Later on, those times start to expand a little bit, you're checking in with people every 12 days, send an email, wait, send an email, wait, and towards the end here, it gets more important because they're starting to run that out of time. They've only got a few days left in their trial and you really want to try and get them to upgrade to a full account before their trial expires. And then finally, an email where they're asking for feedback on the software from the trial user and post-trial nurture list is what they're added to after the very end after they've been sent those emails, very important detail here.

Here's another trigger and an action. If based on the smart segmenting that you can do inside of Autopilot, if they become a paying customer, which means during or at the end of their trial, they upgrade and are now on the paid plan then, so this is if- then, if that, then they are ejected from this journey. Because what happens if someone let's say right here on day 3 or day 15 decides to open up one of your emails and say, you know what fine, I'll click through and I'll go upgrade. They upgrade and they end their trial and they become a paying customer, well you don't want them getting all these emails about how their trials are going. That's a very important part of every workflow, is making sure that you think about all the different possibilities and make sure that your automation is doing what it's supposed to do, which is adapting to all those different possibilities. Adapting to all of those different types of behavior and risk from your customers. The whole nature of these workflows is to be as dynamic as possible, and so don't forget steps like this, removing people from workflows once a desired result has been obtained.

Another one we can look at here is registration follow-up. So when someone registers for let's say a webinar or even a live in-person event, once they've submitted that registration form, you can send them into an audience at Mailchimp is the example here, so an email list. Add them to another list here at Autopilot and send a slack message to your team, letting them know the new person has signed up, add a one day delay and then send an SMS. So this is very basic bare bones reminding them about the event that they registered for, so event registration follow-up. A little bit more advanced would be managing the attendees of a webinar. Now this one's very cool because it segments people based on how they felt after a webinar. So John, how was the webinar after attending? How do you feel about the software after they sat through the webinar and they got three options here, *happy and comfortable*, which they're categorizing as expert. *Okay for now*, which they're categorizing as intermediate, or *I'm still confused and need more help*, and they're labeling that as a beginner. So once that email is sent out, there's a condition which is clicked, and then determining which page was visited, so which of the links were clicked and depending on which one was clicked, then they are sent into different email autoresponder campaigns here. In the case of this one, they're recommending the templates library, they're asking them to sign up for a free trial, and they were added to a list before they were sent those new broadcasts. There's a 15-day delay, and then they're sent a survey and they're asked to fill out a survey, asking how likely would you be to recommend Autopilot to others, and that's another survey software that this directly integrates with. So another cool point for Autopilot there. Then on the intermediate one, there's a video follow-up via email, so if they chose this option here, the 'I'm okay for now', there'll be a video follow-up and then here. 'I'm still confused and need more help', that's a beginner one, if they had clicked on that one, they would have had a completely different experience. They would have been sent into a pipeline with this integration with pipeline here, or they would have been sent a heads-up message. They're going to start getting engaged as a beginner trying to get these people eventually to understand the software more and eventually sign up for it and so on and so forth. So that's managing attendees after a webinar based on what they thought of the webinar, and that's a very cool way to do it.

Another one here, this is very common, possibly the most common automation workflow, at least in the e-commerce space, and that is shopping carts, abandonment and recovery. It's pretty simple, but boy, it really impacts your revenue in a positive way. If you've got a cart abandonment automation workflow set up.

So somebody is sent to a list and the list is based on them abandoning a cart. So they've put in their email address on a shopping cart, but they didn't end up going all the way through the checkout process, so they've been added to that. And the first thing that happens here is they're added to a Facebook audience so that you could do retargeting via Facebook ads, asking them why they didn't check out or reminding them that they still need to purchase so on and so forth. But then there's a one-hour delay from when they were in the cart and didn't purchase, and there's one of those 'you left this behind' emails, you've got those a thousand times. I'm sure I certainly have. You forgot to check out, et cetera, et cetera. Did you forget something? Those are very common subject lines and then there's a four-hour delay again. And then there's an if here, condition, if they visited the cart again and if they have not visited, then you're sending another email saying our team is here to help. So basically just continuing to reach out to them and then see if they need anything else, see if you can sort of nudge them towards making that purchase. A one-day delay here and visiting the page, that's a condition, if they have not visited, then you're doing a split test here, which is another very cool feature of Autopilot. You're sending an abandoned cart discount to half of them, it's a 50, 50 split, so half of them get that, and then the other half get a free shipping offer, so in this case, a discount, a coupon on the actual price. In this case, it's a free shipping offer. And so here, not only are you sending people through a journey that very well could bring them from being a cart abandoner a visitor, a window shopper, if you will, to being a customer. But you're also figuring out which approach leads to the most successful sales. Because you can look at your numbers after this and you can say, hey, the people who got the discount code, the coupon code, they converted at 40%, but the people who were offered no coupon, no discount, but free shipping, they converted at 60%. So the split test functionality inside of Autopilot, as well as other marketing automation software is out there, it is definitely useful. And always be sure to test, test, test.

Here, we've got cart recovered. Once that person has indeed gone back to the cart and finished that initial purchase they were going to make, remove them from the abandoned cart list, remove them from the Facebook audience that you added them to here and eject them from this journey. Eject them from this entire workflow here because you don't want to keep sending them emails saying, hey, why didn't you buy this thing in your cart if they did in fact buy it shortly after being put into this recovery campaign, right? So eject them from this once you've been successful so that they don't continue getting more messages.

And last but not least, we're going to be looking at SMS marketing automation here, and the example that we're using here is hosting an event or a meetup where people can submit their registration via type form. And you add them to an email list here, and you can send them an email here, but more importantly, you're sending them an SMS because presumably you collected their phone number here as well. So you send them an SMS via Twilio, which Autopilot integrates with, and you're just reminding them that they're registered. As you get closer to the event, you're sending simultaneously an email campaign reminding them, but you're also sending them SMSs. Our event is tomorrow, are you still coming? If they reply "Yes", "Great, can't wait to see you here," so there's an acknowledgment of them replying yes. If they're applying "No," "Oh no, you'll be missed, we hope to see you at another one," and then based on that response, segment them to a new list saying not attending versus the list for confirmed registration. And then on the actual day of the event, you've got a time trigger here and that's a very important part of this for events; time trigger. And based on that, if they are on a list or segment, in this case for example, not attending the meetup, pay close attention here, this list is the **not** attending meetup list. So if they are not on that list, if the answer is no, they are not on that list, we want to send them the event reminder because that means they are attending. If they are not on the not attending list, we also send them the SMS saying, hey it's tonight, don't forget to show up.

So that's how they segmented these people, and that's how they responded based on whether or not they had been added way back up here to the not attending meetup which was based on their answer to that SMS. So as you can see, it's pretty complicated, but in a good way, there are all sorts of really cool things that you can do here inside of Autopilot, and these are just a few examples. There are dozens and dozens of different types of workflows that you can create to maximize the power of marketing automation in your business. In the next module, what we're going to be doing is basically starting with a blank canvas and creating a whole workflow automation from scratch.

Module 3

All right, welcome to Module 3. In this module, our expert will show you how to build your first workflow from scratch, so get ready to take some notes and let's jump right in.

All right, so here we are, on our blank canvas we're going to take everything that we've learned so far about automation workflows, and we're going to create our very own right here from scratch. Now, what we're going to create is basically a welcome sequence where we deliver a lead magnet that somebody just opted in for. We're going to try and upsell them to a higher priced offer, and we're going to do a couple of other peripheral things at the same time. So the first thing here is going to be form submitted, we're going to click and drag that over here. And when somebody submits the form on our opt-in page, then the action that we triggered, because that one was a trigger here, the action is going to be that we're going to add them to a list, a corresponding list. You would click here and you would choose the list in question, and the next step is going to be to send an email after they've been added to that list. So send them an email and that email will be the welcome and delivery email. Now, just so you know, inside of Autopilot, all you would basically do in here is either take an existing newsletter or email that you've created, or you would create a new one and a pop-up would show up. And you would basically create your email right here inside of the workflow creation page, which is very handy. But before we go down that email route, we want to do those other two peripheral things that I mentioned. So when somebody submits the form, at the same time as all this other stuff is happening, we're also going to add them to a custom Facebook audience, and we're going to send them an SMS message. We're going to pretend that we had a phone number field on that contact form.

So we'll add them to an SMS list and send them an SMS message, thanking them for their order and telling them to check their email inbox for this email right here. And this email right here, let's go ahead and take advantage of the annotation tools here, just so that we and our team understand and remember what we're seeing. Welcome and delivery, let's call it, we'll just drag that right here, so whenever somebody is looking at this workflow, they understand what this email is. And let's see, let's add a 24-hour delay, let's go ahead and grab this, stick it here on send. So after this email is sent, that'll trigger a 24-hour delay, delay of one day, good, and then after that delay, we're going to set a condition. We're going to see if they have in fact clicked on a link in this welcome email that was sending them to the upsell. Let's go ahead and look for our conditions here, which are at the bottom, and we're going to put 'has visited page', and we're going to grab this and bring it down here. And then from this point forward, where they go in this journey is going to depend on whether or not it was 'no, has not visited' or 'yes has visited,' so this was sort of a fork in the road.

Let's say that they did not visit, we can drag, we're going to put a check email status trigger here. So not visited, we're going to check email status, and if they did not even open that first email... here, so let's go ahead and actually just select this one, that's just a placeholder there, go ahead and publish an exit. So if they did not open email one, which is over here, the welcome and delivery email, if they did not, then we're going to want to re-send that email. Because that happens, sometimes people don't check the welcome email or the delivery email that they just got right after they opted in for something, so you send it a little bit later. In this case, if they have not opened, we send them that email and let's go ahead and annotate that so that we understand, so our team understands what this email is. Re-send welcome, go ahead and put that here, and then if they did open that email, we'll send them a further upsell email, if they did open, and so we'll continue the campaign we're trying to upsell them. Let's go ahead and annotate that as well, just so we know what that email is for.

Now, let's say that they did in fact click the link in this initial email and buy the upsell that we were offering them, that brings us to this question, what is this page here? Where did we put the pixel? We're going to say that this page here is the successful checkout page, so the order confirmation page after they've checked out after purchasing the upsell. So if they have not visited that page, that means they still have not purchased, that's why we're continuing the email experience here, which is ultimately designed to get them to buy. But what if they did end up on that page? Well, if they ended up on that page, that's the indicator to us that they purchased the product in question, and so let's go ahead and do three other things. If they did in fact end up on that page and they purchased, we want to number one, add them to a new list, and that would be a customer list for people who bought the upsell and then number two, we want to remove them from this list. They're no longer just prospects because they've purchased the offer, and finally recall this from Module 2, we saw it in a couple of examples, we'll do it here as well. If they visited, we will eject them from this journey. Remember the launch, if they ended up on this page, an order confirmation page, so if they purchase, then they don't need to continue getting these emails, bothering them about purchasing the thing that they've already purchased. So as soon as they've landed on this page, immediately they would be ejected from this so they don't get any further emails.

And that's it, that's our little email automation experiment here, so let's just recap what we did. Form was submitted some of the opted in for a lead magnet for a free gift of some sort, we added them to a list, at the same moment, we also added them to a Facebook audience. So that in the background behind the scenes here, we could also have been retargeting them with that upsell offer via a Facebook ad. A SMS message reminding them to check their inbox, to actually download the free gift, and we also want them to check because there are links in there offering them the upsell. One day delay, after one day, if they visited that page, which means if they ended up on the order confirmation, so they purchase the upsell, if they did, we remove them from this list, we add them to a new list, which acknowledges that they are a customer, so that's a buyer list there. And then we eject them from this journey and that's it, nothing happens after that point, they are basically cut off right here. But if they did not visit that page after that one day delay, then we go and we check, first, did they even open this initial email? If not, we resend that welcome email, but if they did, we proceed to a marketing email where we focus on selling them on the upsell. And then presumably you could just continue down this path with more email marketing you know, to the right here and so on and so forth, but that's the basics of setting up an email automation, a marketing automation workflow.

Again, it's not just email, as you can see, it's Facebook audiences, it's SMS marketing, a whole lot of other things we could have done here. We could go in here and integrate with that postcard shipping service and have postcards sent to these people depending on what information they submitted in the form. You can do pretty much anything with marketing automation, and hopefully this has helped you get comfortable with the idea marketing automation, because it sounds like a very complex and intimidating topic. As you can see here, thanks to the tools that we have today, such as Autopilot it's drag and drop simple. And frankly, if you're not using it in your business, you are leaving a whole lot of potential money, or potential sales on the table. As you can see, it's easy to do, there's no excuse for not doing it anymore. Take what you've learned in these lessons here, go and apply them with your tool, with your software of choice. Start leveraging marketing automation in your business today.

Don't miss out!

Visit the website below and you can sign up to receive emails whenever B. Vincent publishes a new book. There's no charge and no obligation.

https://books2read.com/r/B-A-QWUO-GFPPB

BOOKS 2 READ

Connecting independent readers to independent writers.

Also by B. Vincent

About the Publisher

Accepting manuscripts in the most categories. We love to help people get their words available to the world.

Revival Waves of Glory focus is to provide more options to be published. We do traditional paperbacks, hardcovers, audio books and ebooks all over the world. A traditional royalty-based publisher that offers self-publishing options, Revival Waves provides a very author friendly and transparent publishing process, with President Bill Vincent involved in the full process of your book. Send us your manuscript and we will contact you as soon as possible.

Contact: Bill Vincent at rwgpublishing@yahoo.com www.rwgpublishing.com